Qty	Form No.	Description		
		All-America		
	1400-ABRS	1987 Medi...		
	300-HBRS	1987 Large...		
	100-GBRS	1988 Cake...		
	100-HBRS	1988 Small Picnic...		
	5400-ABRS	1989 Stitching™	118 B	
	54000-ABRS	1989 Quilting™	150 B	
	10000-OBRS	1990 Small Spoon™	85 B	
	11000-OBRS	1990 Medium Spoon™	91 B	
	12000-OBRS	1990 Mini Waste™	127 B	
	1800-OBRS	1990 Small Waste™	127 B	
	1000-CBRS	1991 Two-quart™ (L)	98 L	
	10707	1992 Small Market™ (L/P)	100 C	
	14541	1993 Liberty™ (L/P)	62 C	
	11134	1994 Candle™ (L/P)	58 C	
	14656	1995 Carry-Along™ (L/P)	63 C	
	31551	1995 Flag Tie-on	12	
	18911	1996 Summertime™ (L/P)		
	32891	1996 Flag Tie-on		
		Bee Baskets™		
	3600-AO	1988 Bee Basket™	119 B	
	5600-BRST	1989 Bee Basket™	135 B	
	3900-AO	1990 Bee Basket™	78 B	
	1500-	1991 Bee Basket™	81 B	
	12335	1992 Bee Basket™	82 B	
	13501	1993 Bee Basket™ (L/P)	99 C	
		1994 Bee Basket™ (L/P)	230 C	
		1994 Bee Tie-on		
		1995 Bee Basket™ (L/P)	222 C	
		1995 Bee Tie-on		
		Booking/Promo Baskets		
		1980 Sunburst		
		19xx-84 Spoon™		
		19xx-84 5" Measuring™		
		19xx-84 Button™		
	1100-AO	1984-90 Candle™	62 B	
	13000-AO	1985-90 Potpourri™	49 B	
	3800-AO	1986-88 Forget-Me-Not™	53 B	
	45000-AO	1988 Sugar and Spice™	57 B	
	45000-IO	1989-90 Keeksake™	48 B	
	13100-JOS	1990-92 Ivy™ (P)	47 P	
	17000-JOS	1990-92 Laurel™ (P)	46 P	
	45000-JOS	1990-92 Rosemary™ (P)	48 P	
	10146	1992-95 Sweet Basil™ (L/P)	42 C	
	209581	1992-95 Potpourri Sachet		
	10102	1992-96 Ambrosia™ (L/P)	39 B	

MW00463043

Qty	Form No.	Description	Market	Cost
Booking/Promo Baskets (Cont.)				
	10138	1992- Lavender™ (L/P)		
	19003	1995- Thyme™ (L/P)		
	15211	1995- Chive™ (L/P)		
Christmas Collection™				
	1100-	1981 Candle Basket™	549 B	
	4900-Z	1982 Granddad Sleigh™	718 B	
	4901-OO	1983 Bell™	511 B	
	4600-AZ	1984 Holly Basket™	319 B	
	5400-A*	1985 Cookie Basket™ (L)	230 L	
	14000-A*T	1986 Candy Cane Basket™	161 B	
	700-A*T	1987 Mistletoe Basket™	107 B	
	3900-B*ST	1988 Poinsettia Basket™	102 B	
	5600-B*ST	1989 Memory Basket™	81 B	
	3400-A*ST	1990 Gingerbread Basket™ (L/P)	103 C	
	5100-C*ST	1991 Yuletide Traditions™ (L/P)	111 C	
	10316/10219	1992 Season's Greetings™ (L/P)	88 C	
	11584/11592	1993 Bayberry™ (L/P)	68 C	
	17906/17914	1994 Jingle Bell™ (L/P)	75 C	
	31437	1994 Jingle Bell Tie-on		
	57908/57916	1994 Jingle Bell Lid		
	19500/19518	1995 Cranberry™ (L/P)	80 C	
	32441	1995 Merry Christmas Tie-on		
	59501/59528	1995 Cranberry Lid		
	23523	1995 Apron		
Collector's Club™				
	62839	1996 Charter Members™ (L/P)		
	150240	1996 Miniature JW Market™ (L/P)	178 B	
Cookie Mold Collection				
	30066	1990 Father Christmas™	75	
		1990 1st Castings™	102	
	30180	1991 Kriss Kringle™	33	
	30457	1992 Santa Claus™	32	
	31062	1993 St. Nick™	27	
	31071	1993 Peace™	33	
	31356	1994 Hope™	24	
	31151	1994 Easter Cookie Mold	26	
	72079	1994 Longaberger Bunnies Book	10	
	31500	1995 Easter Cookie Mold	21	
	72796	1995 Longaberger Bunnies Book		
	32468	1995 Love™		
	32476	1995 Country Cottage™		
	32182	1996 Easter Cookie Mold		

THE
· BENTLEY ·
COLLECTION GUIDE™

The reference tool for consultants, collectors,
and enthusiasts of Longaberger Baskets®

Fourth Edition
1996-1997

Collector's
Checklist

a

j.phillip

INCORPORATED

publication

This inventory checklist is a supplement to **The Bentley Collection Guide™**. The collector edition and specialty baskets are listed alphabetically first in the checklist. Regular line baskets are listed alphabetically the year they were offered.

This checklist allows you to indicate the quantity of baskets you may have, as well as your original cost. The **average** market value for each basket is already printed on the checklist, if available. The values listed for the collector edition and specialty baskets are noted by B (basket only), L (basket sold with liner), P (basket sold with protector), or C (combo). The values for the regular line are for basket only, unless otherwise noted. If any accessories were purchased with the baskets, such as liners or protectors, they can be noted in the description column. Any unique characteristics of the baskets should also be listed, such as special request color weave in earlier baskets.

Market values for regular line baskets are recorded in the year in which the basket was signed. Note that in the regular line listings prior to 1993, some of the baskets do not have current market values listed. Transactions were not obtained for those particular baskets. However, if the basket is still being offered by Longaberger in their current Wish List™, it is valued at least at the current selling price. It should be expected that older baskets are generally worth more than the newer baskets, especially those with the darker stain, which were discontinued around 1986-1987. Two astericks (**) after the form number indicates that the basket was introduced into the regular line in that year.

Copyright© 1996 by James Bentley. Published by **J. Phillip, Incorporated**
5870 Zarley Street - Suite B, New Albany, OH 43054-9700
(800) 837-4394, All rights reserved. This Collector's Checklist may be reproduced once, for insurance purposes only.

ISBN 0-9646280-1-5
ISSN 1082-4790

Qty	Form No.	Description	Market	Cost
		Crisco® American		
	100-DBRS	1991 Crisco Pie™ (P)	365 P	
	10081	1992 Crisco Cookie™ (L/P)	107 C	
		1992 Crisco Apron™	28	
	14745	1993 Crisco Baking™ (L/P)	90 C	
		Easter Series™		
	3500-CX	1987 Medium Chore™	91 B	
	2200-AX	1987 Single Pie™	91 B	
	2300-AX	1987 Small Gathering™	92 B	
	900-AX	1987 Spring™	89 B	
	700-AN	1988 Baby Easter™	70 B	
	3400-AN	1988 Small Easter™	65 B	
	3500-AN	1988 Medium Easter™	70 B	
	3600-AN	1988 Large Easter™	80 B	
	5500-AO	1989 Stained Easter™	74 B	
	5500-ABS	1989 Blue Easter™	82 B	
	5500-APS	1989 Pink Easter™	73 B	
	40000-APVBS	1990 Medium™	67 B	
	41000-APVBS	1990 Large™	72 B	
	900-ATMS	1991 Customer™ (St/Unst)	58 B	
	700-ATMS	1991 Hostess™ (St/Unst)	57 B	
	34000-APVCN	1992 Easter™ (L/P/St/Unst)	60 C	
	10774	1993 Small Easter™(L/P/St/Unst)	61 C	
	13439	1993 Large Easter™(L/P/St/Unst)	67 C	
	16934	1994 Easter™ (L/P)	65 C	
	18708	1995 Easter™ (L/P)	70 C	
	31518	1995 Happy Easter Tie-on	9	
	12912/12939	1996 Easter™ (L/P/St/Unst)		
	32271	1996 Easter Egg Tie-on		
		Employee Baskets™		
	500-	1987 Christmas Med. Market™	235 B	
	100-	1988 Christmas Cake™	131 B	
	1100-	1989 Christmas Candle™	125 B	
	2300-	1990 Christmas Sm. Gathering™	107 B	
	1000-	1991 Christmas Tall Key™	97 B	
	3800-	1992 Christmas 5" Measuring™	83 B	
	5400-	1993 Christmas Button™	81 B	
	700-	1994 Christmas Tea™	89 B	
	10120	1995 Christmas Ambrosia™		
	3800-	1988 Birthday 5" Measuring™	77 B	
	45000-	1989 Birthday Sweetheart™	69 B	
	13000-	1990 Birthday Potpourri™	75 B	
	13100-	1991 Birthday Ivy™	79 B	
	10022	1992 Birthday Tour™	52 B	
		Sophomore Recognition™	51 B	
		Junior Recognition™	67 B	

Qty	Form No.	Description	Market	Cost
		Employee Baskets™ (Cont.)		
		Senior Employee™	80 B	
		Senior Recognition™	85 B	
		Master Recognition™	185 B	
		1994 Perfect Attendance™ (L)		
		1995 Perfect Attendance™ (L)		
		Father's Day™		
	1300-JCWS	1991 Spare Change™ (L/P)	105 C	
	16000	1992 Paper™ (L/P)	87 C	
	15000	1992 Pencil™ (L/P)	92 C	
	18490	1994 Tissue™ (Lid/P)	75 C	
	17477	1994 Business Card™ (P)	65 P	
	11266	1995 Mini Waste™ (L/P/Lid)	76 C	
	12611	1996 Address™ (L/P/Lid/Cards)		
		Feature Baskets (with color)		
	3800-ABS	Resolution™	110 B	
	5600-BBS	Memory™ (book)	128 C	
	17000-AGS	Basket 'O Luck™	103 B	
	300-	Heartland Getaway™	140 B	
	13000-HS	Shamrock™	101 B	
	64408	All-Star Trio™ (L/P)	53	
	190xx	Red Pottery Thank You Basket™	112 B	
	10987	Boo Basket (L/P)	78 C	
	12211	W.T. Pie™ (L/P/Plate)	55 B	
	170xx	1994 R/B/G Small Key™ (P)	33 B	
	151xx	1994 R/B/G Medium Key™ (P)	38 B	
	146xx	1994 R/B/G Tall Key™ (P)	44 B	
	19402	1995 Pumpkin™ (L/P)	91 C	
	59404/59412	1995 Pumpkin/Fall Foliage™ Lid		
	31763	1995 Pumpkin Tie-On	12	
		Feature Baskets (without color)		
	2100-	1981 Bread & Milk™	597 B	
		1982 Old Oak Picnic Basket™	467 B	
	6000-R	1984 Patio Planter™	66 B	
	10000-AO	1984 Shaker Peg Basket™	45 B	
	2200-AO	1984 Single Pie™		
	2300-JO	1985 Pantry™	55 B	
	1000-CO	1985,87 Two-quart™	74 B	
	3200-EO	1985,87 Rd. Sewing (No stand)	157 B	
	1300-AO	1985,88 Small Berry™	29 B	
	1400-AO	1985,88 Medium Berry™	32 B	
	1500-AO	1985,88 Large Berry™	40 B	
	3400-CO	1986 Small Chore™	55 B	
	3500-CO	1986 Medium Chore™	53 B	

Qty	Form No.	Description	Market	Cost
		Feature Baskets (without color) (Cont.)		
	3600-CO	1986 Large Chore™	51 B	
	5500-AN	1986 Daisy™ (Natural)	63 B	
	5500-AO	1986,87 Daisy™ (Stained)	61 B	
	1600-OO	1986 Large Hamper™	157 B	
	4500-AO	1986 Herb™	72 B	
	4600-AO	1986 Garden™	77 B	
	4700-JO	1987 Bakery™	42 B	
	2000-BO	1987 Large Inverted Waste™	120 B	
	500-AN	1987 Medium Market (Natural)		
	2400-CN	1987 Med. Gathering (Natural)		
	200-YO	1987,88 Weekender™	141 B	
	2900-RO	1988 Sm. Planter (w/legs)	120 B	
	3200-RO	1988 Lg. Planter (w/legs)	140 B	
	4500-AO	1989 Bed™ (L)	78 L	
	4700-AO	1989 Breakfast™ (L)	83 L	
	13100-JO	1989 Friendship™	52 B	
	11622	1993,94 Hamper™ (P)	209 P	
		1993 Hostess Appreciation™	64 B	
		1995 Hostess Appreciation™	72 B	
	17124	1995 Horizon of Hope™ (L/P)	52 C	
		Holiday Hostess™		
	2300-JGRS	1987 Tray Basket™	109 B	
	1000-IRGS	1988 Tall Key Basket™	88 B	
	200-YRGS	1988 Weekender™	171 B	
	600-ARGS	1988 Large Market™	114 B	
	2600-ORGS	1988 Small Laundry™	240 B	
	2400-AGRS	1989 Medium Gathering™	104 B	
	3200-BGRS	1989 Large Fruit™	133 B	
	2100-CGRS	1989 Magazine™	117 B	
	4200-CGRS	1990 13" Measuring™	114 B	
	2500-CGRS	1990 Large Gathering™	124 B	
	1900-BRGS	1991 Tree Trimming™ (P)	149 P	
	12700/12718	1992 Gift Giving™ (L/P)	158 C	
	12084/12092	1993 Homecoming™ (L/P)	169 C	
	14427/14435	1994 Sleigh Bell™ (L/P/Lid)	181 C	
	19607/19615	1995 Evergreen™ (L/P/Lid/Div)		
		Hostess Collection™		
	1600-DO	1987-90 Large Hamper™	199 B	
	1700-DO	1987-90 Medium Hamper™	125 B	
	2500-LO	1987-90,91 Doll Cradle™	121 B	
	2800-M	1987-90 Large Cradle™	285 B	
	2800-O	1987-90 Large Laundry™	183 B	
	500-HOS	1990-92 Heirloom™	124 B	
	42000-AOS	1990-92 Hearthside™ (P)	101 P	
	200-YOS	1990-92 Remembrance™ (P)	159 P	

Qty	Form No.	Description	Market	Cost
		Hostess Collection™ (Cont.)		
	3700-AOS	1990-92 Harvest™ (P)	84 P	
	1700-DS	1991 Small Hamper™ (P)	153 B	
	1600-DS	1991 Large Hamper™ (P)	220 B	
	10413	1992-95 Gourmet Picnic™ (L/P)	139 C	
	10600	1992-96 Mail™ (L/P)	113 C	
	60011	1992- Serving Tray™ (L)		
	10111	1992- Wildflower™ (L/P)		
	13234	1995- Sewing (L/P/Lid)		
	14443	1995- Corn (Lid/P)		
	11631	1995- Large Hamper (P)		
	18902	1995- Odds & Ends Basket (P)		
		Incentive/Award Baskets		
		Recruit/Sponsor Baskets:		
	3000-BO	1988 Recruit - Sm. Fruit		
	3100-BO	1988 Recruit - Med. Fruit		
	3200-BO	1988 Recruit - Lg. Fruit		
	13000-BBRS	1988-89 Recruit	161 B	
	1500-BBRS	1988-89 Sponsor	227 B	
	45000-ABRST	1990 Recruit	169 B	
	1100-ABRST	1990 Sponsor	175 B	
	1700-DST	1990-91 Recruit	175 B	
	1600-DST	1990-91 Sponsor	185 B	
	1700-DST	1990-91 Superstar Sponsor		
	10154	1992 Recruit	119 B	
	10162	1992 Sponsor (Large)	118 B	
		1992 Sponsor (Small)		
	16101	1993 Recruit	118 B	
	13323	1993 Sponsor (Large)	123 B	
		1993 Sponsor (Small)	113 B	
		National Sponsoring Award:		
		1992 Natl Recruit Sm. Gathering		
		1992 Natl Recruit Med. Gathering		
		1992 Natl Recruit Lg. Gathering		
		1993 Natl Recruit Sm. Gathering		
		1993 Natl Recruit Med. Gathering		
		1993 Natl Recruit Lg. Gathering		
		1994 Natl Recruit Sm. Gathering		
		1994 Natl Recruit Med. Gathering		
		1994 Natl Recruit Lg. Gathering		
		VIP Baskets:		
		1986 VIP™	350 B	
		1987 VIP™	363 B	
		1988 VIP™	292 B	
		1989 VIP™	313 B	
		1990 VIP™	225 B	
		1991 VIP™	292 B	
		1992 VIP™ (L)	238 B	

Qty	Form No.	Description	Market	Cost
	**Incentive/Award Baskets (Cont.)**				
		1993 VIP™ (L)	285 B	
		1994 VIP™ (L/Handlewrap)	210 B	
		1995 VIP™ (L/Handlewrap)		
		National Sales Awards:		
		1983 High Sales		
		1988 Coverlet		
		1989 Flag		
		1993 Small Fruit		
		1993 Medium Fruit		
		1993 Large Fruit		
		1994 5" Measuring		
		1994 7" Measuring	168 B	
		1994 9" Measuring		
		1994 11" Measuring		
		Miscellaneous Awards/Incentives:		
		1985 Meadow Blossoms Pottery		
	4700-AO	1986 Special Recognition	135 B	
	2300-	1986 Advisor Recognition		
	500-	1987 Tenth Anniversary Market™	170 B	
		1987 Commemorative Plate	108	
	4500-	1987 May Basket (Herb)		
	4500-	1988 Herb™	80 B	
	4600-	1988 Garden™	80 B	
		1988 Herb/Garden Set	138	
		1991 Basket Planter Sleeve™	445 B	
	15000-	1992-Pres Pencil™ — No color	63 B	
	16000-	1992-Pres Paper™ — No color	60 B	
		1992-Pres Pencil/Paper Set	109	
	700-	1993 Holiday Basket of Thanks™	72 B	
		Bee Speaker Baskets:		
	500-	1988 Medium Market		
		1990 Harvest		
	900-	1991 Spring		
	900-	1993 Spring		
	900-	1994 Spring		
	900-	1995 Spring		
		Consultant Advancement Baskets:		
	1000-FO	1988- MBA Basket™	198 B	
		Branch Advisor	260 B	
		Regional Advisor	250 B	
		Director		
		Regional Sponsored Awards:		
	3400-	1991 Small Chore	175 B	
	33000-	1992 Small Oval		
	13000	1993 Potpourri	187 B	
	800-	1994 Small Purse	226 B	
		1995 Medium Berry		
		Directorship Sponsored Awards:		
	45000-	1992 Treasure Chest™	197 B	

Qty	Form No.	Description	Market	Cost
		Incentive/Award Baskets (Cont.)		
		1992 Top Performer		
		1993 Paint the Town™	119 B	
		1993 Top Performer		
		1994 Over the Rainbow™ (Sm.)	121 B	
		1994 Over the Rainbow™ (Med.)	129 B	
		1994 Over the Rainbow™ (Lg.)	152 B	
		1994 Top Performer		
		1995 "Reach for Stars" (Sm.)	167 B	
		1995 "Reach for Stars" (Med.)	185 B	
		1995 "Reach for Stars" (Lg.)		
		1995 High Achiever		
		1996 "Our Business ..." (Sm.)		
		1996 "Our Business ..." (Med.)		
		1996 "Our Business ..." (Lg.)		
		1996 High Achiever		
		J.W. Collection®		
	500-AT	1983 Market Basket™	1163 B	
	1800-OT	1984 Waste Basket™	960 B	
	3200-BT	1985 Apple Basket™	526 B	
	4800-BT	1986 Two-pie Basket™	416 B	
	2100-ABT	1987 Bread and Milk Basket™	406 C	
	2400-ABT	1988 Gathering Basket™	253 B	
	1900-BBST	1989 Banker's Waste Basket™	248 B	
	1500-BBST	1990 Large Berry Basket™ (P)	151 P	
	4400-JBST	1991 Corn Basket™ (P)	324 B	
	100-CBST	1992 Cake Basket™ (L/P)	154 C	
	13722	1993 Original Easter™ (L/P)	135 C	
	11215	1994 Umbrella™ (P)	128 P	
	72214	1994 JW Commemorative Book	25	
		Full Set JW Collection	5680	
		May Series™		
	14000-BVS	1990 Violet™ (L/P)	176 C	
	4700-CSS	1991 Rose™ (L/P)	148 C	
	10006	1992 Pansy™ (L/P)	95 C	
	15717	1993 Lily of the Valley™ (L/P)	69 C	
	16209	1994 Lilac™ (sw/h, L/P)	76 C	
	31291	1994 Lilac™ Tie-on	15	
	14648	1995 Tulip™ (L/P)	72 C	
	31542	1995 Tulip Tie-on	11	
	14915	1995 Sweet Pea™ (L/P)		
	32885	1995 Sweet Pea Tie-on		

Qty	Form No.	Description	Market	Cost
		Mother's Day™		
	11000-BPS	1987 Large Peg™	119 B	
	900-APS	1988 Spring™ (L)	128 L	
	700-APS	1989 Mini Chore™ (L)	100 L	
	33000-JPS	1990 Small Oval™ (L)	87 L	
	800-EPS	1991 Purse™ (sw/h, L/P)	118 C	
	13000-APS	1991 Touch of Pink Potpourri™(L)	71 C	
	110-CPS	1992 Mother's Day™ (L/P)	87 C	
	12904	1993 Mother's Day™ (L/P)	80 C	
	16004	1994 Mother's Day™ (L/P)	71 C	
	72087	1994 Mother's Journal	10	
	18805	1995 Mother's Day™ (L/P)	65 C	
	31470	1995 Mother's Day Tie-on	10	
	14753	1996 Mother's Day (L/P)		
		1996 Mother's Day Lid		
	32328	1996 Mother's Day Tie-on		
		Ornaments		
	70653	Father Christmas™		
	70637	Kriss Kringle™	10	
	70629	Santa Claus™	10	
	70645	St. Nick™		
	70661	Santa Collection set	52	
	72273	1981 Candle		
	72281	1982 Sleigh		
	72290	1983 Bell		
	72303	1984 Holly		
	72311	1994 Baskets Collection Set of 4	48	
	72141	1985 Cookie		
	71838	1986 Candy Cane		
	71943	1987 Mistletoe		
	72460	1988 Poinsetia		
	71803	1995 Baskets Collection Set of 4	48	
		Roseville Pottery		
	30058	Small Mixing Bowl™	40	
	30091	Medium Mixing Bowl™	38	
	30023	Large Mixing Bowl™	52	
	30015	Grandma Bonnie's Pie Plate™	44	
	30082	Small Juice Pitcher™	43	
	30031	Large Milk Pitcher™	58	
		Six-piece Set	225	

Qty	Form No.	Description	Market	Cost
		Retired Baskets		
	4600-OO	(82-88) Bread™ (old)	45 B	
	11002	(79-94) Cake™ (st/h)	48 B	
	16144	(94) Cake™ (Natural)	55 B	
		5" Canister (w/Lid)		
		7" Canister (w/Lid)		
		9" Canister (w/Lid)		
	14401	(79-94) Corn™ (P)	118 P	
	17198	(94) Cracker™ (Natural)	31 B	
	2500-LO	(79-86) Doll Cradle™	163 B	
	2800-MO	(79-86) Large Cradle™	318 B	
	2700-M	(79-86) Medium Cradle™		
	10715	(79-93) Mini Cradle™	55 B	
		(79-80) Small Cradle™		
	15521	(94) Darning™ (Natural)	36 B	
	700-AO	(79-87) Baby Easter™ (st/h)	47 B	
	700-BO	(79-87) Baby Easter™ (sw/h)	56 B	
	3400-AO	(79-87) Small Easter™ (st/h)	49 B	
	3400-BO	(79-87) Small Easter™ (sw/h)	52 B	
	3500-EO	(79-87) Medium Easter™ (st/h)	73 B	
	3500-BO	(79-87) Medium Easter™ (sw/h)	66 B	
	3600-AO	(79-87) Large Easter™ (st/h)	60 B	
	3600-BO	(79-87) Large Easter™ (sw/h)	55 B	
	3000-P	(79-80) Small Hanging Fruit™	77 B	
	3100-P	(79-80) Medium Hanging Fruit™	50 B	
	3200-P	(79-80) Large Hanging Fruit™		
	3300-P	(79-80) Tall Hanging Fruit™		
	13307	(79-95) Tall Fruit™	56 B	
	12301	(86-93) Small Gathering™ (st/h)	74 B	
	12408	(80-93) Med. Gathering™ (st/h)	62 B	
	12505	(83-93) Lg. Gathering™ (st/h) (P)	74 B	
	12513	(79-94) Lg. Gathering™ (2 sw/h)	76 B	
	1600-DO	(79-86) Large Hamper™	211 B	
	1700-DO	(79-86) Medium Hamper™	132 B	
	3800-PO	(80-86) 5" Sq. bottom Hanging™	55 B	
	3900-PO	(80-86) 7" Sq. bottom Hanging™	62 B	
	4000-PO	(80-86) 9" Sq. bottom Hanging™	40 B	
	4100-PO	(80-86) 11" Sq. bottom Hanging™	40 B	
	4200-PO	(80-86) 13" Sq. bottom Hanging™	40 B	
	3700-PO	(80-86) Woven bottom Hanging™	57 B	
	2000-O	(79-84) Lg. Rd. Inv. Waste™	85 B	
	2000-B	(79-84) Lg. Rd. Inv. Waste™ (sw/h)	85 B	
	1900-O	(79-84) Sm. Rd. Inv. Waste™		
	1900-B	(79-84) Sm. Rd. Inv. Waste™ (sw/h)		
	14630	(94) Tall Key™ (Natural)	36 B	
	2800-OO	(79-86) Large Laundry™	182 B	
	2700-O	(79-83) Medium Laundry™		
	10626	(79-93) Large Market™ (st/h)	67 B	
	10421	(79-93) Small Market™ (st/h)	67 B	
	12122	(79-95) Magazine™ (1 sw/h, legs)	83 B	

Qty	Form No.	Description	Market	Cost
		Retired Baskets (Cont.)		
	1600-HO	(83-86) Family Picnic™ (L)	244 B	
	200-H	(79-84) Medium Picnic™	163 B	
	2900-RO	(82-86) Sm. Fern Planter™ (Legs)	97 B	
	2900-SO	(79-86) Sm. Fern Planter™ (13")	115 B	
	2900-TO	(79-86) Sm. Fern Planter™ (20")	77 B	
	3200-RO	(82-86) Lg. Fern Planter™ (Legs)	113 B	
	3200-SO	(79-86) Lg. Fern Planter™ (13")	121 B	
	3200-TO	(79-86) Lg. Fern Planter™ (20")		
	17019	(94) Kiddie Purse™ (Natural)	41 B	
	900-QO	(82-86) Medium Purse™	123 B	
	1000-EO	(79-89) Tall Purse™	117 B	
	3200-NO	(78-86) Round Sewing™ (13")	176 B	
	600-F	(78-83) Rectangular Sewing™	381 B	
	11207	(79-94) Umbrella™	84 P	
	15113	(94) Med. Vegetable™ (Natural)	40 B	
	5200-CO	(83-86) Large Wine™	79 B	
		Shades of Autumn®		
	2200-AGUBS	1990 Pie™	105 B	
	5000-CGUBS	1990 Small Vegetable™	177 B	
	2300-CGUBS	1991 Small Gathering™ (L/P)	137 C	
	700-BGUBS	1991 Acorn™ (L/P)	130 C	
	10804	1992 Bittersweet™ (L/P)	75 C	
	14303	1993 Harvest™ (L/P)	104 C	
	17400	1994 Recipe™ (L/P/Lid)	135 C	
	15563	1995 Basket of Plenty™ (L/P)	109 C	
	59307	1995 Fall Foliage™ Lid		
	31755	1995 Fall Foliage™ Tie-on	9	
		Special Events		
	3800-ABRST	1989 Inaugural™	144 B	
	900-	1989 Bob and Dolores Hope	359 B	
	900-	1990 Bob and Dolores Hope	359 B	
	900-	1991 Bob and Dolores Hope	359 B	
	900-	1992 Bob and Dolores Hope	359 B	
	5700-AO	1992 Discovery™ (L)	77 L	
	900-	1993 Bob and Dolores Hope	359 B	
	11461	1993 Inaugural™ (L/P)	69 C	
	900-	1994 Bob and Dolores Hope	359 B	
	900-	1995 Bob and Dolores Hope	359 B	
	900-	1996 Bob and Dolores Hope	359 B	

Qty	Form No.	Description	Market	Cost
		Sweetheart Baskets™		
	45000-ARS	1990 Sweetheart™ (L)	81 L	
	300-CRS	1990 Sweetheart Getaway™	131 B	
	11347	1993 Sweetheart™ (L/P)	70 C	
	72036	1993 Pewter Sweet Heart Tie-on	20	
	10359	1993 Sweetheart Getaway™(L/P)	138 C	
	18601	1994 Be Mine™ (L/P)	59 C	
		1994 Fabric Heart Tie-on		
	10367	1994 Forever Yours™ (L/P)	138 C	
	19046	1995 Sweet Sentiments™ (L/P)	58 C	
	31780	1995 Small Heart Tie-on		
	10456	1995 Precious Treasures™ (L/P)	168 C	
	31798	1995 Large Heart Tie-on		
		Tour Baskets™		
	5600-BO	1988 Tour™		
	5600-BO	1989 Tour™	58 B	
	5600-BO	1990 Tour™	70 B	
	5600-BO	1991 Tour™	78 B	
	15601	1992 Tour™	49 B	
	15601	1993 Dresden™ (P)	58 P	
	15601	1994 Dresden™ (P)		
	15601	1995 Dresden™ (P)		
	15601	1996 Dresden™ (P)		
	15814	1996 Dresden II™ (P)		
	15601	1995 Hartville (P)		
	15601	1996 Hartville (P)		
		Traditions Collection™		
	19101	1995 Family Basket™ (P)	139 C	
	19119	1995 Community™ (L/P)		
		Wood Products		
		Cupboards:		
		(80) Two-door (pine)	350	
	8101-OO	(84-85) One-door (maple)	301	
	8100-O	(84-85) Two-door (oak)	475	
	8100-OO	(85-86,88) One-door	321	
		Paddles:		
	8010 -O	(83-85) Butte 4-1/2"	31	
	8000-O	1985-94 Butte 6-1/2"		
	8020-OO	(87-88) Heart™	31	
	8030-OO	(87-88) Goose™	22	
	8040-OO	(87-88) Gingerbreadman™	41	
		Wall Hangings:		
	7800-O	(79-84) 10"x14"	75	
	7800-O	(85-86) 12"x16"	125	

Qty	Form No.	Description	Market	Cost
		Wood Products (Cont.)		
	7801-O	(79-80) 12" x 24"		
	7701-O	(79-80) 10" Square	75	
	7700-O	(79-80) 20" Square	168	
	7900-O	(79-80) 12" Triangular		
	7901-A	(79-80) 24" Triangular	95	
	8902-O	(79-85) Large Wall Bracket	33	
	8900-O	(79-85) Small Wall Bracket	30	
		(85-86) Small Wall Bracket		
	7701-X	(80) Framed clock (woven)	345	
	7701-Y	(80) Framed Mirror (woven)	383	
	7701-Z	(80) Picture Frame (woven)		
		(80) Cathedral Mirror	140	
	7900-OO	(85-94) Peg Board™ (w/hearts)	34	
		(N/A) Nail Board		
	8800-O	(79-82) 5" Toilet Paper Holder		
	8801-O	(79-80) 12" Towel Holder	40	
	8802-O	(79-80) 18" Towel Holder		
	8803-O	(79-80) 21" Towel Holder		
	8804-O	(79-80) 24" Towel Holder		
		(80) Bread Box	242	
		(80) Carpenter Box	115	
		(80) Cookbook Nook	172	
		(83-86) Lids for Measuring Baskets		
		(5", 7", 9", 11", 13")		
		(80) Cheese Board		
		(N/A) Wood Scoop		

Qty	Form No.	Description	Market	Cost
		Regular Line — 1979		
	700-J	Mini Berry™ (wooden loops)	50	
	1300-O	Small Berry™	28	
	1300-B	Small Berry™ (sw/h)		
	1400-O	Medium Berry™		
	1400-B	Medium Berry™ (sw/h)		
	1500-O	Large Berry™		
	1500-B	Large Berry™ (sw/h)	45	
	100-A	Cake™ (st/h)	48	
	100-G	Cake™ (st/h, divider)	48	
	4400-O	Corn™	118 P	
	700-K	Mini Cradle™ (wooden loops)	55	
	2500-L	Doll Cradle™	163	
	2600-M	Small Cradle™		
	2700-M	Medium Cradle™		
	2800-M	Large Cradle™	318	
	700-A	Baby Easter™ (st/h)	47	
	700-B	Baby Easter™ (sw/h)	56	
	3400-A	Small Easter™ (st/h)	49	
	3400-B	Small Easter™ (sw/h)	52	
	3500-A	Medium Easter™ (st/h)	73	
	3500-B	Medium Easter™ (sw/h)	66	
	3600-A	Large Easter™ (st/h)	60	
	3600-B	Large Easter™ (sw/h)	55	
	2900-S	Small Fern Planter™ (13" stand)	115	
	2900-T	Small Fern Planter™ (20" stand)	77	
	3200-S	Large Fern Planter™ (13" stand)	121	
	3200-T	Large Fern Planter™ (20" stand)		
	3000-B	Small Fruit™ (sw/h)	45	
	3100-B	Medium Fruit™ (sw/h)		
	3200-B	Large (Apple) Fruit™ (sw/h)	73	
	3300-B	Tall Fruit™ (sw/h)	56	
	2300-C	Small Gathering™ (2 sw/h)	50	
	2400-C	Medium Gathering™ (2 sw/h)		
	2500-C	Large Gathering™ (2 sw/h)	76	
	1600-D	Large Hamper™	211	
	1700-D	Medium Hamper™	132	
	3000-V	Small Hanging™ (hanger)	77	
	3100-P	Medium Hanging™ (hanger)	50	
	3200-P	Large Hanging™ (hanger)		
	3300-P	Tall Hanging™ (hanger)		
	3700-P	Woven bottom Hanging™	57	
	700-I	Small Key™ (wooden loop)	45	
	1100-I	Medium Key™ (wooden loop)	50	
	1000-I	Tall Key™ (wooden loop)		
	2600-O	Small Laundry™		
	2700-O	Medium Laundry™		
	2800-O	Large Laundry™	182	
	2100-C	Magazine™ (2 sw/h)		
	2100-U	Magazine™ (1 sw/h, legs)	83	

Qty	Form No.	Description	Market	Cost
	2100-W	Magazine™ (1 sw/h, lid, legs)		
	400-A	Small Market™ (st/h)	67	
	500-A	Medium Market™ (2 sw/h)		
	600-A	Large Market™ (st/h)	67	
	3800-B	5" Measuring™ (sw/h)	30	
	3900-B	7" Measuring™ (sw/h)		
	4000-B	9" Measuring™ (sw/h)	50	
	4100-B	11" Measuring™ (sw/h)		
	4200-B	13" Measuring™ (sw/h)		
	100-H	Small Picnic™ (2 sw/h, divider)		
	200-H	Medium Picnic™ (2 sw/h, divider)	163	
	300-H	Large Picnic™ (2 sw/h, divider)		
	700-E	Kiddie Purse™ (sw/h, lid)	38	
	800-E	Small Purse™ (sw/h, lid)		
	900-E	Medium Purse™ (sw/h, lid)		
	1000-E	Tall Purse™ (sw/h, lid)	117	
	600-F	Sewing™ Rectangular (2 sw/h)	381	
	3200-N	Sewing™ Round (sw/h,13" stand)	176	
	1200-O	Umbrella™	84 P	
	1700-O	Medium Waste™		
	1800-O	Small Waste™		
	1900-O	Small Inverted Waste™		
	1900-B	Small Inverted Waste™ (sw/h)		
	2000-O	Large Inverted Waste™	85	
	2000-B	Large Inverted Waste™ (sw/h)	85	
		Regular Line — 1980		
	700-JO	Mini Berry™ (wooden loops)	50	
	1300-O	Small Berry™	28	
	1300-B	Small Berry™ (sw/h)		
	1400-O	Medium Berry™		
	1400-B	Medium Berry™ (sw/h)		
	1500-O	Large Berry™		
	1500-B	Large Berry™ (sw/h)	45	
	100-A	Cake™ (st/h)	48	
	100-G	Cake™ (st/h, divider)	48	
	4400-OO	Corn™	118 P	
	700-K	Mini Cradle™ (wooden loops)	55	
	2500-L	Doll Cradle™	163	
	2600-M	Small Cradle™		
	2700-M	Medium Cradle™		
	2800-M	Large Cradle™	318	
	700-A	Baby Easter™ (st/h)	47	
	700-B	Baby Easter™ (sw/h)	56	
	3400-A	Small Easter™ (st/h)	49	
	3400-B	Small Easter™ (sw/h)	52	
	3500-A	Medium Easter™ (st/h)	73	
	3500-B	Medium Easter™ (sw/h)	66	
	3600-A	Large Easter™ (st/h)	60	

Qty	Form No.	Description	Market	Cost
	3600-B	Large Easter™ (sw/h)	55	
	2900-S	Small Fern Planter™ (13" stand)	115	
	2900-T	Small Fern Planter™ (20" stand)	77	
	3200-S	Large Fern Planter™ (13" stand)	121	
	3200-T	Large Fern Planter™ (20" stand)		
	3000-B	Small Fruit™ (sw/h)		
	3100-B	Medium Fruit™ (sw/h)		
	3200-B	Large (Apple) Fruit™ (sw/h)	73	
	3300-B	Tall Fruit™ (sw/h)	56	
	2300-C	Small Gathering™ (2 sw/h)	50	
	2400-C	Medium Gathering™ (2 sw/h)		
	2500-C	Large Gathering™ (2 sw/h)	76	
	1600-D	Large Hamper™	211	
	1700-D	Medium Hamper™	132	
	3000-V	Small Hanging™ (hanger)	77	
	3100-P	Medium Hanging™ (hanger)	50	
	3200-P	Large Hanging™ (hanger)		
	3300-P	Tall Hanging™ (hanger)		
	3700-P	Woven bottom Hanging™	57	
	700-I	Small Key™ (wooden loop)	45	
	1100-I	Medium Key™ (wooden loop)	50	
	1000-I	Tall Key™ (wooden loop)		
	2600-O	Small Laundry™		
	2700-O	Medium Laundry™		
	2800-O	Large Laundry™	182	
	2100-C	Magazine™ (2 sw/h)		
	2100-U	Magazine™ (1 sw/h, legs)	83	
	2100-W	Magazine™ (1 sw/h, lid, legs)		
	400-A	Small Market™ (st/h)	67	
	500-A	Medium Market™ (st/h)		
	600-A	Large Market™ (st/h)	67	
	3800-B	5" Measuring™ (sw/h)	30	
	3900-B	7" Measuring™ (sw/h)		
	4000-B	9" Measuring™ (sw/h)	50	
	4100-B	11" Measuring™ (sw/h)		
	4200-B	13" Measuring™ (sw/h)		
	100-H	Small Picnic™ (2 sw/h, divider)		
	200-H	Medium Picnic™ (2 sw/h, divider)		
	300-H	Large Picnic™ (2 sw/h, divider)		
	700-E	Kiddie Purse™ (sw/h, lid)	38	
	800-E	Small Purse™ (sw/h, lid)		
	900-E	Medium Purse™ (sw/h, lid)		
	1000-E	Tall Purse™ (sw/h, lid)	117	
	600-F	Rectangular Sewing™ (sw/h, lid)	381	
	3200-N	Round Sewing™ (sw/h,13" stand)	176	
	1200-O	Umbrella™	84 P	
	1800-O	Small Waste™		
	1700-O	Medium Waste™		
	1900-O	Small Inverted Waste™		
	1900-B	Small Inverted Waste™ (sw/h)		

Qty	Form No.	Description	Market	Cost
	2000-O	Large Inverted Waste™	85	
	2000-B	Large Inverted Waste™ (sw/h)	85	
		Regular Line — 1981		
	700-JO	Mini Berry™ (wooden loops)	50	
	1300-O	Small Berry™	28	
	1300-B	Small Berry™ (sw/h)		
	1400-O	Medium Berry™		
	1400-B	Medium Berry™ (sw/h)		
	1500-O	Large Berry™		
	1500-B	Large Berry™ (sw/h)	45	
	100-A	Cake™ (st/h)	48	
	100-G	Cake™ (st/h, divider)	48	
	4400-OO	Corn™	118 P	
	700-K	Mini Cradle™ (wooden loops)	55	
	2500-L	Doll Cradle™	163	
	2600-M	Small Cradle™		
	2700-M	Medium Cradle™		
	2800-M	Large Cradle™	318	
	700-A	Baby Easter™ (st/h)	47	
	700-B	Baby Easter™ (sw/h)	56	
	3400-A	Small Easter™ (st/h)	49	
	3400-B	Small Easter™ (sw/h)	52	
	3500-A	Medium Easter™ (st/h)	73	
	3500-B	Medium Easter™ (sw/h)	66	
	3600-A	Large Easter™ (st/h)	49	
	3600-B	Large Easter™ (sw/h)	52	
	2900-S	Small Fern Planter™ (13" stand)	115	
	2900-T	Small Fern Planter™ (20" stand)	77	
	3200-S	Large Fern Planter™ (13" stand)	121	
	3200-T	Large Fern Planter™ (20" stand)		
	3000-B	Small Fruit™ (sw/h)		
	3100-B	Medium Fruit™ (sw/h)		
	3200-B	Large (Apple) Fruit™ (sw/h)	73	
	3300-B	Tall Fruit™ (sw/h)		
	2300-C	Small Gathering™ (2 sw/h)	50	
	2400-C	Medium Gathering™ (2 sw/h)		
	2500-C	Large Gathering™ (2 sw/h)	76	
	1600-D	Large Hamper™	211	
	1700-D	Medium Hamper™	132	
	3700-P	Woven-bottom Hanging™	57	
	3800-P	5" Hanging™	55	
	3900-P	7" Hanging™	62	
	4000-P	9" Hanging™	40	
	4100-P	11" Hanging™	40	
	4200-P	13" Hanging™	40	
	700-I	Small Key™ (wooden loop)	45	
	1100-I	Medium Key™ (wooden loop)	50	
	1000-I	Tall Key™ (wooden loop)		
	2600-O	Small Laundry™		

Qty	Form No.	Description	Market	Cost
	2700-O	Medium Laundry™		
	2800-O	Large Laundry™	182	
	2100-C	Magazine™ (2 sw/h)		
	2100-U	Magazine™ (1 sw/h, legs)	83	
	2100-W	Magazine™ (1 sw/h, lid, legs)		
	400-A	Small Market™ (st/h)	67	
	500-A	Medium Market™ (st/h)		
	600-A	Large Market™ (st/h)	67	
	3800-B	5" Measuring™ (sw/h)		
	3900-B	7" Measuring™ (sw/h)		
	4000-B	9" Measuring™ (sw/h)		
	4100-B	11" Measuring™ (sw/h)		
	4200-B	13" Measuring™ (sw/h)		
	100-H	Small Picnic™ (2 sw/h, divider)		
	200-H	Medium Picnic™ (2 sw/h, divider)	163	
	300-H	Large Picnic™ (2 sw/h, divider)		
	700-E	Kiddie Purse™ (sw/h, lid)	38	
	800-E	Small Purse™ (sw/h, lid)		
	900-E	Medium Purse™ (sw/h, lid)		
	1000-E	Tall Purse™ (sw/h, lid)	117	
	600-F	Sewing™Rectangular (sw/h, lid)	381	
	3200-N	Sewing™ Round (sw/h,13" stand)	176	
	1200-O	Umbrella™	84 P	
	1800-O	Small Waste™		
	1700-O	Medium Waste™		
	1900-O	Small Inverted Waste™		
	1900-B	Small Inverted Waste™ (sw/h)		
	2000-O	Large Inverted Waste™	85	
	2000-B	Large Inverted Waste™ (sw/h)	85	
		Regular Line — 1982		
	700-JO	Mini Berry™ (wooden loops)		
	1300-O	Small Berry™		
	1300-B	Small Berry™ (sw/h)		
	1400-O	Medium Berry™		
	1400-B	Medium Berry™ (sw/h)		
	1500-O	Large Berry™		
	1500-B	Large Berry™ (sw/h)		
	100-A	Cake™ (st/h)	48	
	100-G	Cake™ (st/h, divider)	48	
	4400-OO	Corn™	118 P	
	700-K	Mini Cradle™ (wooden loops)	55	
	2500-L	Doll Cradle™	163	
	2600-M	Small Cradle™		
	2700-M	Medium Cradle™		
	2800-M	Large Cradle™	318	
	700-A	Baby Easter™ (st/h)	47	
	700-B	Baby Easter™ (sw/h)	56	
	3400-A	Small Easter™ (st/h)	49	
	3400-B	Small Easter™ (sw/h)	52	

Qty	Form No.	Description	Market	Cost
	3500-A	Medium Easter™ (st/h)	73	
	3500-B	Medium Easter™ (sw/h)	60	
	3600-A	Large Easter™ (st/h)	60	
	3600-B	Large Easter™ (sw/h)	55	
	2900-S	Small Fern Planter™ (13" stand)	115	
	2900-T	Small Fern Planter™ (20" stand)	77	
	3200-S	Large Fern Planter™ (13" stand)	121	
	3200-T	Large Fern Planter™ (20" stand)		
	3000-B	Small Fruit™ (sw/h)		
	3100-B	Medium Fruit™ (sw/h)		
	3200-B	Large (Apple) Fruit™ (sw/h)	73	
	3300-B	Tall Fruit™ (sw/h)	56	
	2300-C	Small Gathering™ (2 sw/h)	50	
	2400-A	Medium Gathering™ (st/h)	62	
	2400-C	Medium Gathering™ (2 sw/h)		
	2500-A	Large Gathering™ (st/h)	74	
	2500-C	Large Gathering™ (2 sw/h)	76	
	1600-D	Large Hamper™	211	
	1700-D	Medium Hamper™	132	
	3700-P	Woven-bottom Hanging™	57	
	3800-P	5" Hanging™	55	
	3900-P	7" Hanging™	62	
	4000-P	9" Hanging™		
	4100-P	11" Hanging™		
	4200-P	13" Hanging™		
	700-I	Small Key™ (wooden loop)	45	
	1100-I	Medium Key™ (wooden loop)	50	
	1000-I	Tall Key™ (wooden loop)		
	2600-O	Small Laundry™		
	2700-O	Medium Laundry™		
	2800-O	Large Laundry™	182	
	2100-C	Magazine™ (2 sw/h)		
	2100-U	Magazine™ (1 sw/h, legs)	83	
	2100-W	Magazine™ (1 sw/h, lid, legs)		
	400-A	Small Market™ (st/h)	67	
	500-A	Medium Market™ (st/h)		
	600-A	Large Market™ (st/h)	67	
	3800-B	5" Measuring™ (sw/h)	30	
	3900-B	7" Measuring™ (sw/h)		
	4000-B	9" Measuring™ (sw/h)	50	
	4100-B	11" Measuring™ (sw/h)		
	4200-B	13" Measuring™ (sw/h)		
	100-H	Small Picnic™ (2 sw/h, divider)		
	200-H	Medium Picnic™ (2 sw/h, divider)	163	
	300-H	Large Picnic™ (2 sw/h, divider)		
	700-E	Kiddie Purse™ (sw/h, lid)	38	
	800-E	Small Purse™ (sw/h, lid)		
	900-E	Medium Purse™ (sw/h, lid)		
	1000-E	Tall Purse™ (sw/h, lid)	117	
	600-F	Sewing™ Rectangular (sw/h, lid)	381	

Qty	Form No.	Description	Market	Cost
	3200-N	Sewing™ Round (sw/h,13" stand)	176	
	1200-O	Umbrella™	84 P	
	1800-O	Small Waste™		
	1700-O	Medium Waste™		
	1900-O	Small Inverted Waste™		
	1900-B	Small Inverted Waste™ (sw/h)		
	2000-O	Large Inverted Waste™	85	
	2000-B	Large Inverted Waste™ (sw/h)	85	
		Regular Line - 1983		
	700-JO	Mini Berry™ (wooden loops)	50	
	1300-O	Small Berry™	28	
	1300-B	Small Berry™ (sw/h)		
	1400-O	Medium Berry™		
	1400-B	Medium Berry™ (sw/h)		
	1500-O	Large Berry™		
	1500-B	Large Berry™ (sw/h)	40	
	4600-O**	Bread™ (old)	45	
	100-G	Cake™ (st/h, divider)	48	
	4400-O	Corn™	118 P	
	4500-O**	Cracker™	35	
	700-K	Mini Cradle™ (wooden loops)	55	
	2500-L	Doll Cradle™	163	
	2800-M	Large Cradle™	318	
	5500-J**	Darning™	45	
	700-A	Baby Easter™ (st/h)	47	
	700-B	Baby Easter™ (sw/h)	56	
	3400-A	Small Easter™ (st/h)	49	
	3400-B	Small Easter™ (sw/h)	52	
	3500-A	Medium Easter™ (st/h)	73	
	3500-B	Medium Easter™ (sw/h)	60	
	3600-A	Large Easter™ (st/h)	60	
	3600-B	Large Easter™ (sw/h)	55	
	2900-RO**	Small Fern Planter™ (legs)	97	
	2900-S	Small Fern Planter™ (13" stand)	115	
	2900-T	Small Fern Planter™ (20" stand)	77	
	3200-RO**	Large Fern Planter™ (legs)	113	
	3200-S	Large Fern Planter™ (13" stand)	121	
	3200-T	Large Fern Planter™ (20" stand)		
	3000-B	Small Fruit™ (sw/h)		
	3100-B	Medium Fruit™ (sw/h)		
	3200-B	Large (Apple) Fruit™ (sw/h)	73	
	3300-B	Tall Fruit™ (sw/h)	56	
	2300-C	Small Gathering™ (2 sw/h)	50	
	2400-A	Medium Gathering™ (st/h)	62	
	2400-C	Medium Gathering™ (2 sw/h)		
	2500-A	Large Gathering™ (st/h)	74	
	2500-C	Large Gathering™ (2 sw/h)	76	
	1600-D	Large Hamper™	211	
	1700-D	Small Hamper™	132	

Qty	Form No.	Description	Market	Cost
	3700-P	Woven-bottom Hanging™	57	
	3800-P	5" Hanging™	55	
	3900-P	7" Hanging™	62	
	4000-P	9" Hanging™	40	
	4100-P	11" Hanging™	40	
	4200-P	13" Hanging™	40	
	700-I	Small Key™ (wooden loop)	45	
	1100-I	Medium Key™ (wooden loop)	50	
	1000-I	Tall Key™ (wooden loop)		
	2600-O	Small Laundry™		
	2800-O	Large Laundry™	182	
	2100-C	Magazine™ (2 sw/h)	75	
	2100-U	Magazine™ (1 sw/h, legs)	83	
	2100-W	Magazine™ (1 sw/h, lid, legs)	75	
	400-A	Small Market™ (st/h)	67	
	500-A	Medium Market™ (st/h)		
	600-A	Large Market™ (st/h)	67	
	3800-B	5" Measuring™ (sw/h)	30	
	3900-B	7" Measuring™ (sw/h)		
	4000-B	9" Measuring™ (sw/h)	50	
	4100-B	11" Measuring™ (sw/h)		
	4200-B	13" Measuring™ (sw/h)		
	100-H	Small Picnic™ (2 sw/h, divider)		
	200-H	Medium Picnic™ (2 sw/h, divider)	163	
	300-H	Large Picnic™ (2 sw/h, divider)		
	2600-HO**	Family Picnic™ (L) (2 sw/h)	244	
	700-E	Kiddie Purse™ (sw/h, lid)	38	
	800-E	Small Purse™ (sw/h, lid)		
	900-E	Medium Purse™ (sw/h, lid)		
	900-Q**	Medium Purse™ (st/h, split lid)	123	
	1000-E	Tall Purse™ (sw/h, lid)	117	
	3200-N	Sewing™ Round (sw/h,13" stand)	176	
	11000-O**	Medium Spoon™		
	900-A**	Spring™ (st/h)	75	
	1200-O	Umbrella™	84 P	
	5000-O**	Small Vegetable™	40	
	5100-C**	Medium Vegetable™ (2 sw/h)		
	5200-CO**	Large Wine™ (2 sw/h, divider)	79	
	1800-O	Small Waste™		
	1700-O	Medium Waste™		
	12000-O	Mini Waste™		
	1900-O	Small Inverted Waste™		
	1900-B	Small Inverted Waste™ (sw/h)		
	2000-O	Large Inverted Waste™	85	
	2000-B	Large Inverted Waste™ (sw/h)	85	
	Regular Line — 1984			
	700-JO	Mini Berry™ (leather loops)		
	1300-O	Small Berry™	28	
	1300-B	Small Berry™ (sw/h)		

Qty	Form No.	Description	Market	Cost
	1400-O	Medium Berry™		
	1400-B	Medium Berry™ (sw/h)		
	1500-O	Large Berry™		
	1500-B	Large Berry™ (sw/h)	40	
	4600-O	Bread™ (old)	45	
	5400-O**	Button™	30	
	100-G	Cake™ (st/h, divider)	48	
	4400-O	Corn™	118 P	
	4500-O	Cracker™		
	700-M	Mini Cradle™ (loops removed)	55	
	2500-L	Doll Cradle™	163	
	2800-M	Large Cradle™	318	
	5500-J	Darning™	45	
	700-A	Baby Easter™ (st/h)	47	
	700-B	Baby Easter™ (sw/h)	56	
	3400-A	Small Easter™ (st/h)	49	
	3400-B	Small Easter™ (sw/h)	52	
	3500-A	Medium Easter™ (st/h)	73	
	3500-B	Medium Easter™ (sw/h)	60	
	3600-A	Large Easter™ (st/h)	60	
	3600-B	Large Easter™ (sw/h)	55	
	2900-R	Small Fern Planter™ (legs)	97	
	2900-S	Small Fern Planter™ (13" stand)	115	
	2900-T	Small Fern Planter™ (20" stand)	77	
	3200-R	Large Fern Planter™ (legs)	113	
	3200-S	Large Fern Planter™ (13" stand)	121	
	3200-T	Large Fern Planter™ (20" stand)		
	3000-B	Small Fruit™ (sw/h)		
	3100-B	Medium Fruit™ ((sw/h)		
	3200-B	Large (Apple) Fruit™ (sw/h)	73	
	3300-B	Tall Fruit™ (sw/h)	56	
	2300-C	Small Gathering™ (2 sw/h)	50	
	2400-A	Medium Gathering™ (st/h)	62	
	2400-C	Medium Gathering™ (2 sw/h)		
	2500-A	Large Gathering™ (st/h)	74	
	2500-C	Large Gathering™ (2 sw/h)	76	
	1600-D	Large Hamper™	211	
	1700-D	Small Hamper™	132	
	3700-P	Woven bottom Hanging™	57	
	3800-P	5" Hanging™	55	
	3900-P	7" Hanging™	62	
	4000-P	9" Hanging™	40	
	4100-P	11" Hanging™	40	
	4200-P	13" Hanging™	40	
	700-I	Small Key™ (leather loop)		
	1100-I	Medium Key™ (leather loop)		
	1000-I	Tall Key™ (leather loop)		
	2600-O	Small Laundry™		
	2800-O	Large Laundry™	182	
	2100-C	Magazine™ (2 sw/h)		

Qty	Form No.	Description	Market	Cost
	2100-U	Magazine™ (1 sw/h, legs)	83	
	2100-W	Magazine™ (1 sw/h, lid, legs)		
	400-A	Small Market™ (st/h)	67	
	500-A	Medium Market™ (st/h)		
	500-C	Medium Market™ (2 sw/h)		
	600-A	Large Market™ (st/h)	67	
	600-C	Large Market™ (2 sw/h)		
	3800-B	5" Measuring™ (sw/h)	30	
	3900-B	7" Measuring™ (sw/h)		
	4000-B	9" Measuring™ (sw/h)	50	
	4100-B	11" Measuring™ (sw/h)		
	4200-B	13" Measuring™ (sw/h)		
	100-H	Small Picnic™ (2 sw/h, divider)		
	300-H	Large Picnic™ (2 sw/h, divider)		
	2600-H	Family Picnic™ (L) (2 sw/h, lid)	244	
	700-E	Kiddie Purse™ (sw/h, lid)	38	
	800-E	Small Purse™ (sw/h, lid)		
	900-E	Medium Purse™ (sw/h, lid)		
	900-O	Medium Purse™ (st/h, split lid)	123	
	1000-E	Tall Purse™ (sw/h, lid)	117	
	3200-N	Sewing™ Round (sw/h,13" stand)	176	
	10000-O**	Small Spoon™		
	11000-O	Medium Spoon™	50	
	900-A	Spring™ (st/h)	75	
	1200-O	Umbrella™	84 P	
	5000-O	Small Vegetable™		
	5100-C	Medium Vegetable™ (2 sw/h)		
	1800-O	Small Waste™		
	1700-O	Medium Waste™		
	12000-O	Mini Waste™		
	5200-C	Large Wine™ (2 sw/h, divider)	85	
		Regular Line — 1985		
	700-JO	Mini Berry™ (leather loops)		
	1300-O	Small Berry™	28	
	1300-B	Small Berry™ (sw/h)		
	1400-O	Medium Berry™		
	1400-B	Medium Berry™ (sw/h)		
	1500-O	Large Berry™		
	1500-B	Large Berry™ (sw/h)	40	
	4600-O	Bread™ (old)	45	
	5400-O	Button™	30	
	100-G	Cake™ (st/h, divider)	48	
	4400-O	Corn™	118 P	
	4500-O	Cracker™		
	700-M	Mini Cradle™	55	
	2500-L	Doll Cradle™	163	
	2800-M	Large Cradle™	318	
	5500-J	Darning™	45	
	700-A	Baby Easter™ (st/h)	47	

Qty	Form No.	Description	Market	Cost
	700-B	Baby Easter™ (sw/h)	56	
	3400-A	Small Easter™ (st/h)	49	
	3400-B	Small Easter™ (sw/h)	52	
	3500-A	Medium Easter™ (st/h)	73	
	3500-B	Medium Easter™ (sw/h)	60	
	3600-A	Large Easter™ (st/h)	60	
	3600-B	Large Easter™ (sw/h)	55	
	2900-R	Small Fern Planter™ (legs)	97	
	2900-S	Small Fern Planter™ (13" stand)	115	
	2900-T	Small Fern Planter™ (20" stand)	77	
	3200-R	Large Fern Planter™ (legs)	113	
	3200-S	Large Fern Planter™ (13" stand)	121	
	3200-T	Large Fern Planter™ (20" stand)		
	3000-B	Small Fruit™ (sw/h)		
	3100-B	Medium Fruit™ ((sw/h)		
	3200-B	Large (Apple) Fruit™ (sw/h)	73	
	3300-B	Tall Fruit™ (sw/h)	56	
	2300-C	Small Gathering™ (2 sw/h)	50	
	2400-A	Medium Gathering™ (st/h)	62	
	2400-C	Medium Gathering™ (2 sw/h)	50	
	2500-A	Large Gathering™ (st/h)	74	
	2500-C	Large Gathering™ (2 sw/h)	76	
	1600-D	Large Hamper™	211	
	1700-D	Small Hamper™	132	
	3700-P	Woven bottom Hanging™	57	
	3800-P	5" Hanging™	55	
	3900-P	7" Hanging™	62	
	4000-P	9" Hanging™	40	
	4100-P	11" Hanging™	40	
	4200-P	13" Hanging™	40	
	700-I	Small Key™ (leather loop)		
	1100-I	Medium Key™ (leather loop)		
	1000-I	Tall Key™ (leather loop)		
	2600-O	Small Laundry™		
	2800-O	Large Laundry™	182	
	2100-C	Magazine™ (2 sw/h)		
	2100-U	Magazine™ (1 sw/h, legs)	83	
	2100-W	Magazine™ (1 sw/h, lid, legs)		
	400-A	Small Market™ (st/h)	67	
	500-A	Medium Market™ (st/h)		
	500-C	Medium Market™ (2 sw/h)		
	600-A	Large Market™ (st/h)	67	
	600-C	Large Market™ (2 sw/h)		
	3800-B	5" Measuring™ (sw/h)	30	
	3900-B	7" Measuring™ (sw/h)		
	4000-B	9" Measuring™ (sw/h)	50	
	4100-B	11" Measuring™ (sw/h)		
	4200-B	13" Measuring™ (sw/h)		
	100-H	Small Picnic™ (2 sw/h, divider)		
	300-H	Large Picnic™ (2 sw/h, divider)		

Qty	Form No.	Description	Market	Cost
	2600-H	Family Picnic™ (L) (2 sw/h, lid)	244	
	700-E	Kiddie Purse™ (sw/h, lid)	38	
	800-E	Small Purse™ (sw/h, lid)		
	900-E	Medium Purse™ (sw/h, lid)		
	900-O	Medium Purse™ (sw/h, split lid)	123	
	1000-E	Tall Purse™ (sw/h, lid)	117	
	3200-N	Sewing™ Round (sw/h,13" stand)	176	
	11000-O	Medium Spoon™		
	900-A	Spring™ (st/h)	75	
	1200-O	Umbrella™	84 P	
	5000-O	Small Vegetable™		
	5100-C	Medium Vegetable™ (2 sw/h)		
	12000-O	Mini Waste™		
	1800-O	Small Waste™		
	1700-O	Medium Waste™		
	5200-C	Large Wine™ (2 sw/h, divider)	85	
		Regular Line — 1986		
	700-JO	Mini Berry™		
	1300-O	Small Berry™	28	
	1300-B	Small Berry™ (sw/h)		
	1400-O	Medium Berry™		
	1400-B	Medium Berry™ (sw/h)		
	1500-O	Large Berry™		
	1500-B	Large Berry™ (sw/h)	40	
	4600-O	Bread™ (old)	45	
	5400-JO	Button™	30	
	100-C**	Cake™ (2 sw/h, divider)		
	100-G	Cake™ (st/h, divider)	48	
	3500-CO**	Medium Chore™ (2 sw/h)		
	4400-O	Corn™	118 P	
	4500-O	Cracker™		
	700-M	Mini Cradle™	55	
	2500-L	Doll Cradle™	163	
	2800-M	Large Cradle™	318	
	5500-J	Darning™	45	
	700-A	Baby Easter™ (st/h)	47	
	700-B	Baby Easter™ (sw/h)	56	
	3400-A	Small Easter™ (st/h)	49	
	3400-B	Small Easter™ (sw/h)	52	
	3500-A	Medium Easter™ (st/h)	73	
	3500-B	Medium Easter™ (sw/h)	60	
	3600-A	Large Easter™ (st/h)	60	
	3600-B	Large Easter™ (sw/h)	55	
	2900-R	Small Fern Planter™ (legs)	97	
	2900-S	Small Fern Planter™ (13" stand)	115	
	2900-T	Small Fern Planter™ (20" stand)	77	
	3200-R	Large Fern Planter™ (legs)	113	
	3200-S	Large Fern Planter™ (13" stand)	121	
	3200-T	Large Fern Planter™ (20" stand)		

Qty	Form No.	Description	Market	Cost
	3000-B	Small Fruit™ (sw/h)		
	3100-B	Medium Fruit™ (sw/h)		
	3200-B	Large (Apple) Fruit™ (sw/h)	73	
	3300-B	Tall Fruit™ (sw/h)	56	
	2300-A	Small Gathering™ (st/h)	74	
	2300-C	Small Gathering™ (2 sw/h)	50	
	2400-A	Medium Gathering™ (st/h)	62	
	2400-C	Medium Gathering™ (2 sw/h)		
	2500-A	Large Gathering™ (st/h)	74	
	2500-C	Large Gathering™ (2 sw/h)	76	
	1600-D	Large Hamper™	211	
	1700-D	Small Hamper™	132	
	3700-P	Woven bottom Hanging™	57	
	3800-P	5" Hanging™	55	
	3900-P	7" Hanging™	62	
	4000-P	9" Hanging™	40	
	4100-P	11" Hanging™	40	
	4200-P	13" Hanging™	40	
	700-I	Small Key™		
	1100-I	Medium Key™		
	1000-I	Tall Key™		
	2600-O	Small Laundry™		
	2800-O	Large Laundry™	182	
	2100-C	Magazine™ (2 sw/h)		
	2100-U	Magazine™ (1 sw/h, legs)	83	
	2100-W	Magazine™ (1 sw/h, lid, legs)		
	400-A	Small Market™ (st/h)	67	
	500-A	Medium Market™ (st/h)		
	500-C	Medium Market™ (2 sw/h)		
	600-A	Large Market™ (st/h)	67	
	600-C	Large Market™ (2 sw/h)		
	3800-B	5" Measuring™ (sw/h)	30	
	3900-B	7" Measuring™ (sw/h)		
	4000-B	9" Measuring™ (sw/h)	50	
	4100-B	11" Measuring™ (sw/h)		
	4200-B	13" Measuring™ (sw/h)		
	2300-J**	Pantry™ (ears)		
	14000-A**	Small Peg™ (st/h)	30	
	10000-A**	Medium Peg™ (st/h)		
	11000-A**	Large Peg™ (st/h)		
	100-H	Small Picnic™ (2 sw/h, divider)		
	300-H	Large Picnic™ (2 sw/h, divider)		
	2600-H	Family Picnic™ (L) (2 sw/h)	244	
	2200-O**	Pie™ (st/h)		
	700-E	Kiddie Purse™ (sw/h, lid)	38	
	800-E	Small Purse™ (sw/h, lid)		
	900-E	Medium Purse™ (sw/h, lid)		
	900-Q	Medium Purse™ (sw/h, split lid)	123	
	1000-E	Tall Purse™ (sw/h, lid)	117	
	3200-N	Sewing™ Round (sw/h, 13" stand)	176	

Qty	Form No.	Description	Market	Cost
	10000-O	Small Spoon™		
	11000-O	Medium Spoon™		
	900-A	Spring™ (st/h)	75	
	1200-O	Umbrella™	84 P	
	5000-O	Small Vegetable™	35	
	5100-C	Medium Vegetable™ (2 sw/h)		
	5200-C	Large Vegetable™ (2 sw/h)		
	12000-O	Mini Waste™		
	1800-O	Small Waste™		
	1700-O	Medium Waste™		
		Regular Line — 1987		
	700-JO	Mini Berry™		
	1300-O	Small Berry™	28	
	1300-B	Small Berry™ (sw/h)		
	1400-O	Medium Berry™		
	1400-B	Medium Berry™ (sw/h)		
	1500-O	Large Berry™		
	1500-B	Large Berry™ (sw/h)	40	
	4600-O	Bread™ (old)	45	
	5400-JO	Button™		
	100-C	Cake™ (2 sw/h, divider)		
	100-G	Cake™ (st/h, divider)	48	
	3500-CO	Medium Chore™ (2 sw/h)		
	4400-O	Corn™	118 P	
	4500-O	Cracker™		
	700-M	Mini Cradle™	55	
	5500-J	Darning™		
	3000-B	Small Fruit™ (sw/h)		
	3100-B	Medium Fruit™ (sw/h)		
	3200-B	Large (Apple) Fruit™ (sw/h)		
	3300-B	Tall Fruit™ (sw/h)	56	
	2300-A	Small Gathering™ (st/h)	74	
	2300-C	Small Gathering™ (2 sw/h)		
	2400-A	Medium Gathering™ (st/h)	62	
	2400-C	Medium Gathering™ (2 sw/h)		
	2500-A	Large Gathering™ (st/h)	74	
	2500-C	Large Gathering™ (2 sw/h)	76	
	700-I	Small Key™		
	1100-I	Medium Key™		
	1000-I	Tall Key™		
	2600-O	Small Laundry™		
	2100-C	Magazine™ (2 sw/h)		
	2100-U	Magazine™ (1 sw/h, legs)	83	
	2100-W	Magazine™ (1 sw/h, lid, legs)		
	400-A	Small Market™ (st/h)	67	
	500-A	Medium Market™ (st/h)		
	500-C	Medium Market™ (2 sw/h)		
	600-A	Large Market™ (st/h)	67	
	600-C	Large Market™ (2 sw/h)		

Qty	Form No.	Description	Market	Cost
	3800-B	5" Measuring™ (sw/h)		
	3900-B	7" Measuring™ (sw/h)	40	
	4000-B	9" Measuring™ (sw/h)		
	4100-B	11" Measuring™ (sw/h)		
	4200-B	13" Measuring™ (sw/h)		
	2300-J	Pantry™ (2 ears)		
	14000-A	Small Peg™ (st/h)		
	10000-A	Medium Peg™ (st/h)		
	11000-A	Large Peg™ (st/h)		
	100-H	Small Picnic™ (2 sw/h, divider)		
	300-H	Large Picnic™ (2 sw/h, divider)		
	2200-O	Pie™ (st/h)		
	700-E	Kiddie Purse™ (sw/h, lid)	38	
	800-E	Small Purse™ (sw/h, lid)		
	900-E	Medium Purse™ (sw/h, lid)		
	1000-E	Tall Purse™ (sw/h, lid)	117	
	10000-O	Small Spoon™		
	11000-O	Medium Spoon™		
	900-A	Spring™ (st/h)		
	1200-O	Umbrella™	84 P	
	5000-O	Small Vegetable™		
	5100-C	Medium Vegetable™ (2 sw/h)		
	5200-C	Large Vegetable™ (2 sw/h)		
	12000-O	Mini Waste™		
	1800-O	Small Waste™		
	1700-O	Medium Waste™		
		Regular Line — 1988		
	700-JO	Mini Berry™		
	1300-O	Small Berry™	28	
	1300-B	Small Berry™ (sw/h)		
	1400-O	Medium Berry™		
	1400-B	Medium Berry™ (sw/h)		
	1500-O	Large Berry™		
	1500-B	Large Berry™ (sw/h)	40	
	4700-O**	Bread™ (new)		
	5400-JO	Button™		
	100-C	Cake™ (2 sw/h, divider)		
	100-G	Cake™ (st/h, divider)	48	
	3500-CO	Medium Chore™ (2 sw/h)		
	4400-O	Corn™	118 P	
	4500-O	Cracker™		
	700-M	Mini Cradle™	55	
	5500-J	Darning™		
	3000-B	Small Fruit™ (sw/h)		
	3100-B	Medium Fruit™ (sw/h)		
	3200-B	Large (Apple) Fruit™ (sw/h)		
	3300-B	Tall Fruit™ (sw/h)	56	
	2300-A	Small Gathering™ (st/h)	74	
	2300-C	Small Gathering™ (2 sw/h)		

Qty	Form No.	Description	Market	Cost
	2400-A	Medium Gathering™ (st/h)	62	
	2400-C	Medium Gathering™ (2 sw/h)		
	2500-A	Large Gathering™ (st/h)	74	
	2500-C	Large Gathering™ (2 sw/h)	76	
	700-I	Small Key™		
	1100-I	Medium Key™		
	1000-I	Tall Key™		
	2600-O	Small Laundry™		
	2100-C	Magazine™ (2 sw/h)		
	2100-U	Magazine™ (1 sw/h, legs)	83	
	2100-W	Magazine™ (1 sw/h, lid, legs)		
	400-A	Small Market™ (st/h)	67	
	500-A	Medium Market™ (st/h)		
	500-C	Medium Market™ (2 sw/h)		
	600-A	Large Market™ (st/h)	67	
	600-C	Large Market™ (2 sw/h)		
	3800-B	5" Measuring™ (sw/h)		
	3900-B	7" Measuring™ (sw/h)		
	4000-B	9" Measuring™ (sw/h)		
	4100-B	11" Measuring™ (sw/h)		
	4200-B	13" Measuring™ (sw/h)		
	2300-J	Pantry™ (2 ears)		
	14000-A	Small Peg™ (st/h)		
	10000-A	Medium Peg™ (st/h)		
	11000-A	Large Peg™ (st/h)		
	100-H	Small Picnic™ (2 sw/h, divider)		
	300-H	Large Picnic™ (2 sw/h, divider)		
	2200-O	Pie™ (st/h)		
	700-E	Kiddie Purse™ (sw/h, lid)		
	800-E	Small Purse™ (sw/h, lid)		
	900-E	Medium Purse™ (sw/h, lid)		
	1000-E	Tall Purse™ (sw/h, lid)	117	
	10000-O	Small Spoon™		
	11000-O	Medium Spoon™		
	900-A	Spring™ (st/h)		
	1200-O	Umbrella™	84 P	
	5000-O	Small Vegetable™		
	5100-C	Medium Vegetable™ (2 sw/h)		
	5200-C	Large Vegetable™ (2 sw/h)		
	12000-O	Mini Waste™		
	1800-O	Small Waste™		
	1700-O	Medium Waste™		
		Regular Line — 1989		
	700-JO	Mini Berry™		
	1300-O	Small Berry™		
	1300-B	Small Berry™ (sw/h)		
	1400-O	Medium Berry™		
	1400-B	Medium Berry™ (sw/h)		
	1500-O	Large Berry™		

Qty	Form No.	Description	Market	Cost
	1500-B	Large Berry™ (sw/h)		
	4700-O	Bread™ (new)		
	5400-JO	Button™		
	100-C	Cake™ (2 sw/h, divider)		
	100-G	Cake™ (st/h, divider)	48	
	3500-CO	Medium Chore™ (2 sw/h)		
	4400-O	Corn™	118 P	
	4500-O	Cracker™		
	700-M	Mini Cradle™	55	
	5500-J	Darning™		
	3000-B	Small Fruit™ (sw/h)		
	3100-B	Medium Fruit™ (sw/h)		
	3200-B	Large (Apple) Fruit™ (sw/h)		
	3300-B	Tall Fruit™ (sw/h)	56	
	2300-A	Small Gathering™ (st/h)	74	
	2300-C	Small Gathering™ (2 sw/h)		
	2400-A	Medium Gathering™ (st/h)	62	
	2400-C	Medium Gathering™ (2 sw/h)		
	2500-A	Large Gathering™ (st/h)	74	
	2500-C	Large Gathering™ (2 sw/h)	76	
	700-I	Small Key™		
	1100-I	Medium Key™		
	1000-I	Tall Key™		
	2600-O	Small Laundry™		
	2100-C	Magazine™ (2 sw/h)		
	2100-U	Magazine™ (1 sw/h, legs)	83	
	2100-W	Magazine™ (1 sw/h, lid, legs)		
	400-A	Small Market™ (st/h)	67	
	500-A	Medium Market™ (st/h)		
	500-C	Medium Market™ (2 sw/h)		
	600-A	Large Market™ (st/h)	67	
	600-C	Large Market™ (2 sw/h)		
	3800-B	5" Measuring™ (sw/h)		
	3900-B	7" Measuring™ (sw/h)		
	4000-B	9" Measuring™ (sw/h)		
	4100-B	11" Measuring™ (sw/h)		
	4200-B	13" Measuring™ (sw/h)		
	2300-J	Pantry™ (2 ears)		
	14000-A	Small Peg™ (st/h)		
	10000-A	Medium Peg™ (st/h)		
	11000-A	Large Peg™ (st/h)		
	100-H	Small Picnic™ (2 sw/h, divider)		
	300-H	Large Picnic™ (2 sw/h, divider)		
	2200-O	Pie™ (st/h)		
	700-E	Kiddie Purse™ (sw/h, lid)		
	800-E	Small Purse™ (sw/h, lid)		
	900-E	Medium Purse™ (sw/h, lid)		
	1000-E	Tall Purse™ (sw/h, lid)	117	
	10000-O	Small Spoon™		
	11000-O	Medium Spoon™		

Qty	Form No.	Description	Market	Cost
	900-A	Spring™ (st/h)	45	
	1200-O	Umbrella™	84 P	
	5000-O	Small Vegetable™		
	5100-C	Medium Vegetable™ (2 sw/h)		
	5200-C	Large Vegetable™ (2 sw/h)		
	12000-O	Mini Waste™		
	1800-O	Small Waste™		
	1700-O	Medium Waste™		
		Regular Line — 1990		
	700-JO	Mini Berry™		
	1300-O	Small Berry™		
	1300-B	Small Berry™ (sw/h)		
	1400-O	Medium Berry™		
	1400-B	Medium Berry™ (sw/h)		
	1500-O	Large Berry™		
	1500-B	Large Berry™ (sw/h)		
	4700-O	Bread™ (new)		
	5400-JO	Button™		
	100-C	Cake™ (2 sw/h, divider)		
	100-G	Cake™ (st/h, divider)	48	
	3500-CO	Medium Chore™ (2 sw/h)		
	4400-O	Corn™	118 P	
	4500-O	Cracker™		
	700-M	Mini Cradle™	55	
	5500-J	Darning™		
	3000-B	Small Fruit™ (sw/h)		
	3100-B	Medium Fruit™ (sw/h)		
	3200-B	Large (Apple) Fruit™ (sw/h)		
	3300-B	Tall Fruit™ (sw/h)	56	
	2300-A	Small Gathering™ (st/h)	74	
	2300-C	Small Gathering™ (2 sw/h)		
	2400-A	Medium Gathering™ (st/h)	62	
	2400-C	Medium Gathering™ (2 sw/h)		
	2500-A	Large Gathering™ (st/h)	74	
	2500-C	Large Gathering™ (2 sw/h)	76	
	700-I	Small Key™		
	1100-I	Medium Key™		
	1000-I	Tall Key™		
	2600-O	Small Laundry™		
	2100-C	Magazine™ (2 sw/h)		
	2100-U	Magazine™ (1 sw/h, legs)	83	
	2100-W	Magazine™ (1 sw/h, lid, legs)		
	400-A	Small Market™ (st/h)	67	
	500-A	Medium Market™ (st/h)		
	500-C	Medium Market™ (2 sw/h)		
	600-A	Large Market™ (st/h)	67	
	600-C	Large Market™ (2 sw/h)		
	3800-B	5" Measuring™ (sw/h)		
	3900-B	7" Measuring™ (sw/h)		

Qty	Form No.	Description	Market	Cost
	4000-B	9" Measuring™ (sw/h)		
	4100-B	11" Measuring™ (sw/h)		
	4200-B	13" Measuring™ (sw/h)		
	2300-J	Pantry™ (2 ears)		
	14000-A	Small Peg™ (st/h)		
	10000-A	Medium Peg™ (st/h)		
	11000-A	Large Peg™ (st/h)		
	100-H	Small Picnic™ (2 sw/h, divider)		
	300-H	Large Picnic™ (2 sw/h, divider)		
	2200-O	Pie™ (st/h)		
	700-E	Kiddie Purse™ (sw/h, lid)		
	800-E	Small Purse™ (sw/h, lid)		
	900-E	Medium Purse™ (sw/h, lid)		
	10000-O	Small Spoon™		
	11000-O	Medium Spoon™		
	900-A	Spring™ (st/h)	45	
	1200-O	Umbrella™	84 P	
	5000-O	Small Vegetable™		
	5100-C	Medium Vegetable™ (2 sw/h)		
	5200-C	Large Vegetable™ (2 sw/h)		
	12000-O	Mini Waste™		
	1800-O	Small Waste™		
	1700-O	Medium Waste™		
		Regular Line — 1991		
	700-JO	Mini Berry™		
	1300-O	Small Berry™		
	1300-B	Small Berry™ (sw/h)		
	1400-O	Medium Berry™		
	1400-B	Medium Berry™ (sw/h)		
	1500-O	Large Berry™		
	1500-B	Large Berry™ (sw/h)		
	4700-O	Bread™ (new)		
	5400-JO	Button™		
	100-C	Cake™ (2 sw/h, divider)		
	100-G	Cake™ (st/h, divider)	48	
	3500-CO	Medium Chore™ (2 sw/h)		
	4400-O	Corn™	118 P	
	4500-O	Cracker™		
	700-M	Mini Cradle™	55	
	5500-J	Darning™		
	3000-B	Small Fruit™ (sw/h)		
	3100-B	Medium Fruit™ (sw/h)		
	3200-B	Large (Apple) Fruit™ (sw/h)		
	3300-B	Tall Fruit™ (sw/h)	56	
	2300-A	Small Gathering™ (st/h)	74	
	2300-C	Small Gathering™ (2 sw/h)		
	2400-A	Medium Gathering™ (st/h)	62	
	2400-C	Medium Gathering™ (2 sw/h)		
	2500-A	Large Gathering™ (st/h)	74	

Qty	Form No.	Description	Market	Cost
	2500-C	Large Gathering™ (2 sw/h)	76	
	700-I	Small Key™		
	1100-I	Medium Key™		
	1000-I	Tall Key™		
	2600-O	Small Laundry™		
	2100-C	Magazine™ (2 sw/h)		
	2100-U	Magazine™ (1 sw/h, legs)	83	
	2100-W	Magazine™ (1 sw/h, lid, legs)		
	400-A	Small Market™ (st/h)	67	
	500-A	Medium Market™ (st/h)		
	500-C	Medium Market™ (2 sw/h)		
	600-A	Large Market™ (st/h)	67	
	600-C	Large Market™ (2 sw/h)		
	3800-B	5" Measuring™ (sw/h)		
	3900-B	7" Measuring™ (sw/h)		
	4000-B	9" Measuring™ (sw/h)		
	4100-B	11" Measuring™ (sw/h)		
	4200-B	13" Measuring™ (sw/h)		
	2300-J	Pantry™ (2 ears)		
	14000-A	Small Peg™ (st/h)		
	10000-A	Medium Peg™ (st/h)		
	11000-A	Large Peg™ (st/h)		
	100-H	Small Picnic™ (2 sw/h, divider)		
	300-H	Large Picnic™ (2 sw/h, divider)		
	2200-O	Pie™ (st/h)		
	700-E	Kiddie Purse™ (sw/h, lid)		
	800-E	Small Purse™ (sw/h, lid)		
	900-E	Medium Purse™ (sw/h, lid)		
	10000-O	Small Spoon™		
	11000-O	Medium Spoon™		
	900-A	Spring™ (st/h)	45	
	1200-O	Umbrella™	84 P	
	5000-O	Small Vegetable™		
	5100-C	Medium Vegetable™ (2 sw/h)		
	5200-C	Large Vegetable™ (2 sw/h)		
	12000-O	Mini Waste™		
	1800-O	Small Waste™		
	1700-O	Medium Waste™		
		Regular Line — 1992		
	11304	Small Berry™		
	11312	Small Berry™ (sw/h)		
	11410	Medium Berry™		
	11428	Medium Berry™ (sw/h)		
	11509	Large Berry™		
	11517	Large Berry™ (sw/h)		
	14702	Bread™ (New)		
	15407	Button™		
	11002	Cake™ (st/h, divider)		
	1011	Cake™ (2 sw/h, divider)	48	

Qty	Form No.	Description	Market	Cost
	13511	Medium Chore™ (2 sw/h)		
	14401	Corn™	118 P	
	14508	Cracker™		
	10715	Mini Cradle™	55	
	15504	Darning™		
	13005	Small Fruit™ (sw/h)		
	13102	Medium Fruit™ (sw/h)		
	13200	Large (Apple) Fruit™ (sw/h)		
	13307	Tall Fruit™ (sw/h)	56	
	12301	Small Gathering™ (st/h)	74	
	12319	Small Gathering™ (2 sw/h)		
	12408	Medium Gathering™ (st/h)	62	
	12416	Medium Gathering™ (2 sw/h)		
	12505	Large Gathering™ (st/h)	74	
	12513	Large Gathering™ (2 sw/h)	76	
	10723	Small Key™		
	11100	Medium Key™		
	11053	Tall Key™		
	12602	Small Laundry™		
	12106	Magazine™ (2 sw/h)		
	12122	Magazine™ (1 sw/h, legs)	83	
	12114	Magazine™ (1 sw/h, lid, legs)		
	10421	Small Market™ (st/h)	67	
	10529	Medium Market™ (sth)		
	10537	Medium Market™ (2 sw/h)		
	10626	Large Market™ (st/h)	67	
	10634	Large Market™ (2 sw/h)		
	13803	5" Measuring™ (sw/h)		
	13901	7" Measuring™ (sw/h)		
	14001	9" Measuring™ (sw/h)		
	14109	11" Measuring™ (sw/h)		
	14206	13" Measuring™ (sw/h)		
	12327	Pantry™ (2 ears)		
	11452	Small Peg™ (st/h)		
	11070	Medium Peg™ (st/h)		
	11151	Large Peg™ (st/h)		
	11029	Small Picnic™ (2 sw/h, divider)		
	10324	Large Picnic™ (2 sw/h, divider)		
	12203	Pie™ (st/h)		
	10731	Kiddie Purse™ (sw/h, lid)		
	10821	Small Purse™ (sw/h, lid)		
	10901	Medium Purse™ (sw/h, lid)		
	11088	Small Spoon™		
	11169	Medium Spoon™		
	10928	Spring™ (st/h)		
	10740†	Tea™	100	
	11207	Umbrella™		
	15008	Small Vegetable™		
	15105	Medium Vegetable™ (2 sw/h)		
		† Name changed from Mini Berry		

Qty	Form No.	Description	Market	Cost
	15202	Large Vegetable™ (2 sw/h)		
	11258	Mini Waste™		
	11801	Small Waste™		
	11703	Medium Waste™		
		Regular Line — 1993		
	11304	Small Berry™		
	11312	Small Berry™ (sw/h)		
	11410	Medium Berry™		
	11428	Medium Berry™ (sw/h)		
	11509	Large Berry™		
	11517	Large Berry™ (sw/h)		
	14702	Bread™ (New)		
	15407	Button™		
	11002	Cake™ (st/h, divider)	48	
	11011	Cake™ (2 sw/h, divider)		
	13510	Medium Chore™ (2 sw/h)		
	14401	Corn™	118 P	
	14508	Cracker™		
	15504	Darning™		
	13005	Small Fruit™ (sw/h)		
	13102	Medium Fruit™ (sw/h)		
	13200	Large (Apple) Fruit™ (sw/h)		
	13307	Tall Fruit™ (sw/h)	56	
	12319	Small Gathering™ (2 sw/h)		
	12416	Medium Gathering™ (2 sw/h)		
	12513	Large Gathering™ (2 sw/h)	76	
	10723	Small Key™		
	11100	Medium Key™		
	11053	Tall Key™		
	12602	Small Laundry™		
	12106	Magazine™ (2 sw/h)		
	12122	Magazine™ (1 sw/h, legs)	83	
	12114	Magazine™ (1 sw/h, lid, legs)		
	10430	Small Market™ (2 sw/h)		
	10529	Medium Market™ (st/h)		
	10537	Medium Market™ (2 sw/h)		
	10634	Large Market™ (2 sw/h)		
	13803	5" Measuring™ (sw/h)		
	13901	7" Measuring™ (sw/h)		
	14001	9" Measuring™ (sw/h)		
	14109	11" Measuring™ (sw/h)		
	14206	13" Measuring™ (sw/h)		
	12327	Pantry™ (2 ears)		
	11452	Small Peg™ (st/h)		
	11070	Medium Peg™ (st/h)		
	11151	Large Peg™ (st/h)		
	11029	Small Picnic™ (2 sw/h, divider)		
	10324	Large Picnic™ (2 sw/h, divider)		
	12203	Pie™ (st/h)		

Qty	Form No.	Description	Market	Cost
	10731	Kiddie Purse™ (sw/h, lid)		
	10821	Small Purse™ (sw/h, lid)		
	10901	Medium Purse™ (sw/h, lid)		
	11088	Small Spoon™		
	11169	Medium Spoon™		
	10928	Spring™ (st/h)		
	10740	Tea™		
	11207	Umbrella™	84 P	
	15008	Small Vegetable™		
	15105	Medium Vegetable™ (2 sw/h)		
	15202	Large Vegetable™ (2 sw/h)		
	11258	Mini Waste™		
	11801	Small Waste™		
	11703	Medium Waste™		
		Regular Line — 1994		
	11304	Small Berry™		
	11312	Small Berry™ (sw/h)		
	11410	Medium Berry™		
	11428	Medium Berry™ (sw/h)		
	11509	Large Berry™		
	11517	Large Berry™ (sw/h)		
	14702	Bread™ (New)		
	15407	Button™		
	11011	Cake™ (2 sw/h, divider)		
	13510	Medium Chore™ (2 sw/h)		
	14508	Cracker™		
	15504	Darning™		
	16306**	Flower Pot Basket™ (loops)		
	13005	Small Fruit™ (sw/h)		
	13102	Medium Fruit™ (sw/h)		
	13200	Large (Apple) Fruit™ (sw/h)		
	13307	Tall Fruit™ (sw/h)	56	
	12319	Small Gathering™ (2 sw/h)		
	12416	Medium Gathering™ (2 sw/h)		
	10723	Small Key™		
	11100	Medium Key™		
	11053	Tall Key™		
	12602	Small Laundry™		
	12106	Magazine™ (2 sw/h)		
	12122	Magazine™ (1 sw/h, legs)	83	
	12114	Magazine™ (1 sw/h, lid, legs)		
	10430	Small Market™ (2 sw/h)		
	10529	Medium Market™ (st/h)		
	10537	Medium Market™ (2 sw/h)		
	10634	Large Market™ (2 sw/h)		
	13803	5" Measuring™ (sw/h)		
	13901	7" Measuring™ (sw/h)		
	14001	9" Measuring™ (sw/h)		
	14109	11" Measuring™ (sw/h)		

Qty	Form No.	Description	Market	Cost
	14206	13" Measuring™ (sw/h)		
	12327	Pantry™		
	11452	Small Peg™ (st/h)		
	11070	Medium Peg™ (st/h)		
	11151	Large Peg™ (st/h)		
	11029	Small Picnic™ (sw/h, divider)		
	10324	Large Picnic™ (sw/h, divider)		
	12203	Pie™ (st/h)		
	10731	Kiddie Purse™ (sw/h, lid)		
	10821	Small Purse™ (sw/h, lid)		
	10901	Medium Purse™ (sw/h, lid)		
	11088	Small Spoon™		
	11169	Medium Spoon™		
	10928	Spring™ (st/h)		
	10740	Tea™		
	15008	Small Vegetable™		
	15105	Medium Vegetable™ (2 sw/h)		
	15202	Large Vegetable™ (2 sw/h)		
	11258	Mini Waste™		
	11801	Small Waste™		
	11703	Medium Waste™		
		Regular Line -- 1995		
	11304	Small Berry™		
	11312	Small Berry™ (sw/h)		
	11410	Medium Berry™		
	11428	Medium Berry™ (sw/h)		
	11509	Large Berry™		
	11517	Large Berry™ (sw/h)		
	14702	Bread™ (New)		
	15407	Button™		
	11011	Cake™ (2 sw/h, divider)		
	13510	Medium Chore™ (2 sw/h)		
	14508	Cracker™		
	15504	Darning™		
	16306	Flower Pot Basket™ (loops)		
	13005	Small Fruit™ (sw/h)		
	13102	Medium Fruit™ (sw/h)		
	13200	Large (Apple) Fruit™ (sw/h)		
	12319	Small Gathering™ (2 sw/h)		
	12416	Medium Gathering™ (2 sw/h)		
	10723	Small Key™		
	11100	Medium Key™		
	11053	Tall Key™		
	12602	Small Laundry™		
	12106	Magazine™ (2 sw/h)		
	12114	Magazine™ (1 sw/h, lid, legs)		
	10430	Small Market™ (2 sw/h)		
	10529	Medium Market™ (st/h)		
	10537	Medium Market™ (2 sw/h)		

Qty	Form No.	Description	Market	Cost
	10634	Large Market™ (2 sw/h)		
	13803	5" Measuring™ (sw/h)		
	13901	7" Measuring™ (sw/h)		
	14001	9" Measuring™ (sw/h)		
	14109	11" Measuring™ (sw/h)		
	14206	13" Measuring™ (sw/h)		
	12327	Pantry™		
	11452	Small Peg™ (st/h)		
	11070	Medium Peg™ (st/h)		
	11151	Large Peg™ (st/h)		
	11029	Small Picnic™ (sw/h, divider)		
	10324	Large Picnic™ (sw/h, divider)		
	12203	Pie™ (st/h)		
	10731	Kiddie Purse™ (sw/h, lid)		
	10821	Small Purse™ (sw/h, lid)		
	10901	Medium Purse™ (sw/h, lid)		
	11088	Small Spoon™		
	11169	Medium Spoon™		
	10928	Spring™ (st/h)		
	10740	Tea™		
	15008	Small Vegetable™		
	15105	Medium Vegetable™ (2 sw/h)		
	15202	Large Vegetable™ (2 sw/h)		
	11258	Mini Waste™		
	11801	Small Waste™		
	11703	Medium Waste™		
		Regular Line -- 1996		
	11304	Small Berry™	22.95	
	11312	Small Berry™ (sw/h)	25.95	
	11410	Medium Berry™	24.95	
	11428	Medium Berry™ (sw/h)	27.95	
	11509	Large Berry™	30.95	
	11517	Large Berry™ (sw/h)	33.95	
	14702	Bread™ (New)	30.95	
	15407	Button™	25.95	
	11011	Cake™ (2 sw/h, divider)	53.95	
	13510	Medium Chore™ (2 sw/h)	41.95	
	14508	Cracker™	23.95	
	15504	Darning™	35.95	
	18414	Flower Pot Basket, Small (loops)	34.95	
	16306	Flower Pot Basket™ (loops)	48.95	
	13005	Small Fruit™ (sw/h)	29.95	
	13102	Medium Fruit™ (sw/h)	35.95	
	13200	Large (Apple) Fruit™ (sw/h)	59.95	
	12319	Small Gathering™ (2 sw/h)	48.95	
	12416	Medium Gathering™ (2 sw/h)	61.95	
	10723	Small Key™	24.95	
	11100	Medium Key™	27.95	

Qty	Form No.	Description	Market	Cost
	11053	Tall Key™	36.95	
	12602	Small Laundry™	133.95	
	12106	Magazine™ (2 sw/h)	69.95	
	12114	Magazine™ (1 sw/h, lid, legs)	79.95	
	10430	Small Market™ (2 sw/h)	50.95	
	10529	Medium Market™ (st/h)	50.95	
	10537	Medium Market™ (2 sw/h)	60.95	
	10634	Large Market™ (2 sw/h)	68.95	
	13803	5" Measuring™ (sw/h)	26.95	
	13901	7" Measuring™ (sw/h)	34.95	
	14001	9" Measuring™ (sw/h)	42.95	
	14109	11" Measuring™ (sw/h)	50.95	
	14206	13" Measuring™ (sw/h)	68.95	
	12327	Pantry™	40.95	
	11452	Small Peg™ (st/h)	26.95	
	11070	Medium Peg™ (st/h)	28.95	
	11151	Large Peg™ (st/h)	34.95	
	11029	Small Picnic™ (sw/h, divider)	68.95	
	10324	Large Picnic™ (sw/h, divider)	102.95	
	12203	Pie™ (st/h)	39.95	
	10731	Kiddie Purse™ (sw/h, lid)	34.95	
	10821	Small Purse™ (sw/h, lid)	44.95	
	10901	Medium Purse™ (sw/h, lid)	49.95	
	17418	Recipe™	29.95	
	11088	Small Spoon™	24.95	
	11169	Medium Spoon™	30.95	
	10928	Spring™ (st/h)	36.95	
	10740	Tea™	23.95	
	15008	Small Vegetable™	30.95	
	15105	Medium Vegetable™ (2 sw/h)	45.95	
	15202	Large Vegetable™ (2 sw/h)	54.95	
	11258	Mini Waste™	41.95	
	11801	Small Waste™	53.95	
	11703	Medium Waste™	81.95	
		Heartland® Collection		
	14711	Bakery™ (leather ears)	37.95	
	15423	Button™ (leather ears)	31.95	
	10758	Mini Chore™ (1 st/h)	27.95	
	13404	Small Chore™ (1 st/h)	29.95	
	13528	Medium Chore™ (1 st/h)	46.95	
	15598	Darning (2 ears)	39.95	
	10782	Small Key™ (leather loop)	28.95	
	1118	Medium Key™ (leather loop)	30.95	
	11061	Tall Key™ (leather loop)	41.95	
	10545	Medium Market™ (1 st/h)	58.95	
	14516	Muffin™ (leather ears)	27.95	
	11177	Large Peg™ (1 st/h)	36.95	
	10839	Small Purse™ (1 sw/h, lid)	47.95	

Qty	Form No.	Description	Market	Cost
	11096	Small Spoon™	27.95	
	10936	Spring™ (1 st/h)	40.95	
	Woven Traditions™			
	11533	Large Berry™	34.95	
	14737	Bread™	37.95	
	11657	Cake	59.95	
	14532	Cracker™	27.95	
	15539	Darning™ (leather ears)	39.95	
	11142	Large Peg	40.95	
	19038	Spring	42.95	
	10710	Tea™ (leather ears)	29.95	
	15016	Small Vegetable™	36.95	

j.phillip inc.
5870 Zarley Street, Suite B
New Albany, OH 43054-9700
(800) 837-4394

ISBN 0-9646280-1-5